Plants are Wonderful

A Coloring Book

By Michael Reed

Copyright @2016 by MR

Acknowledgement

I thank God for giving me the interest for this coloring book.

Plants are some of the wonderful organisms on Earth.

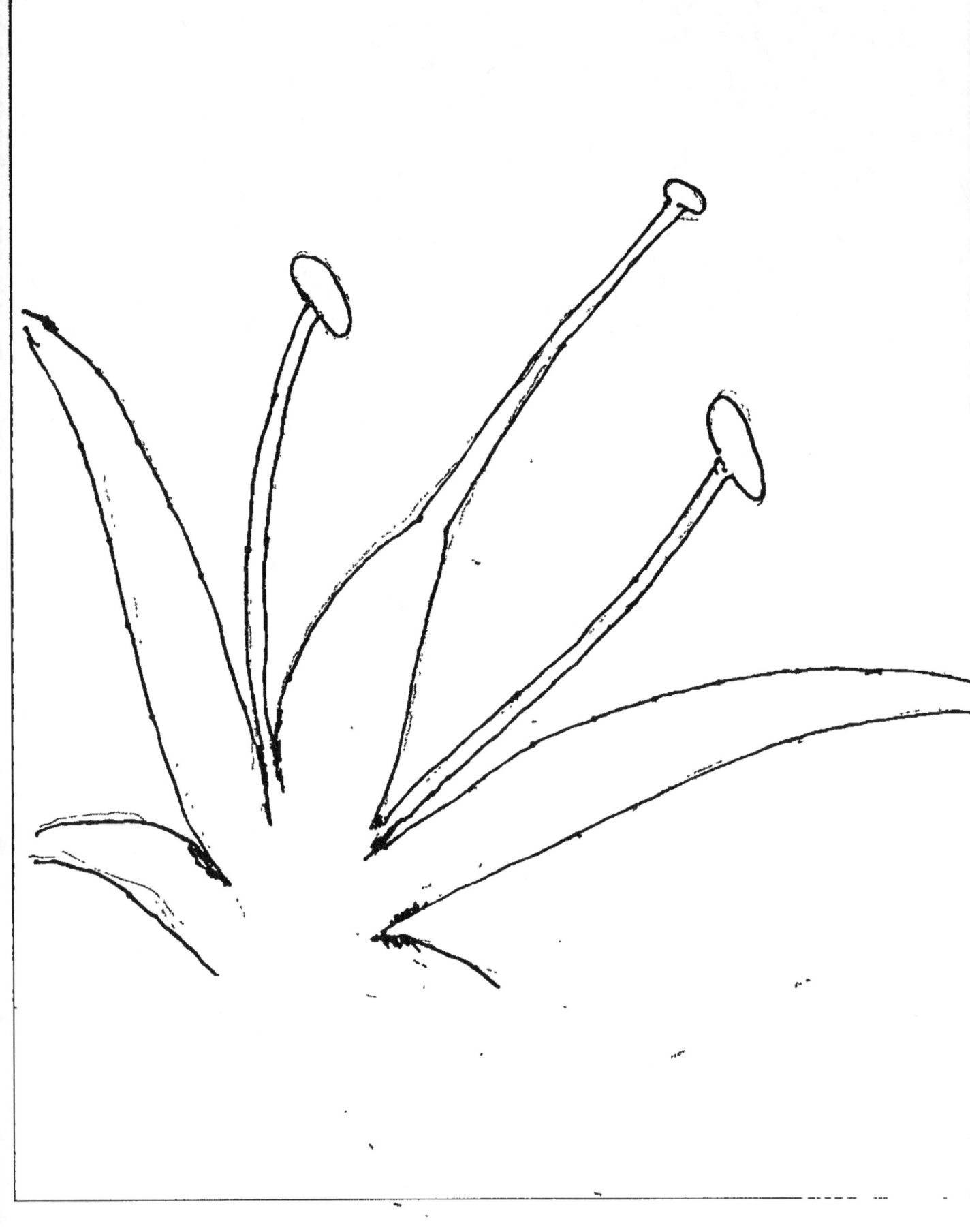

Plants come in many forms.

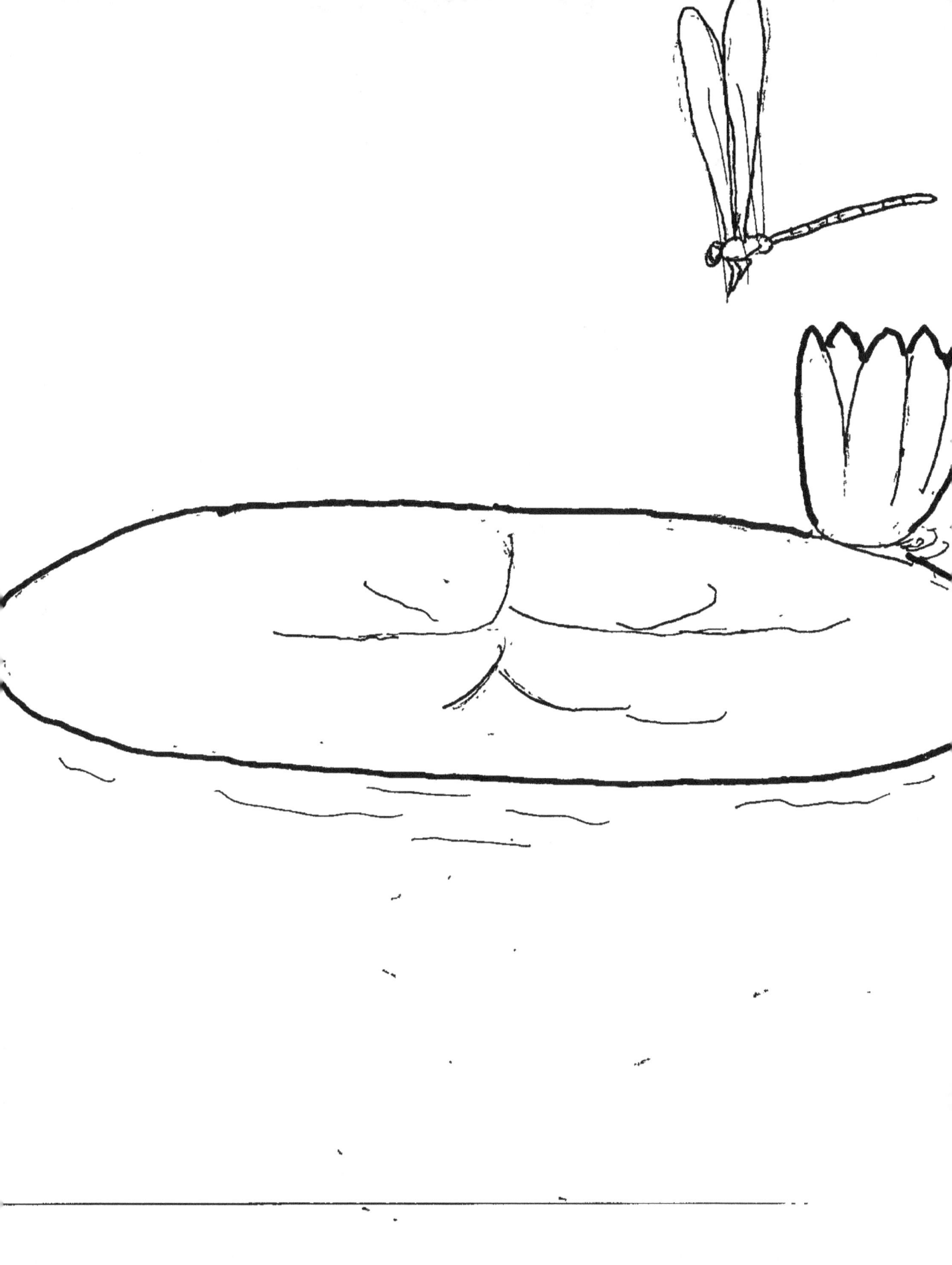

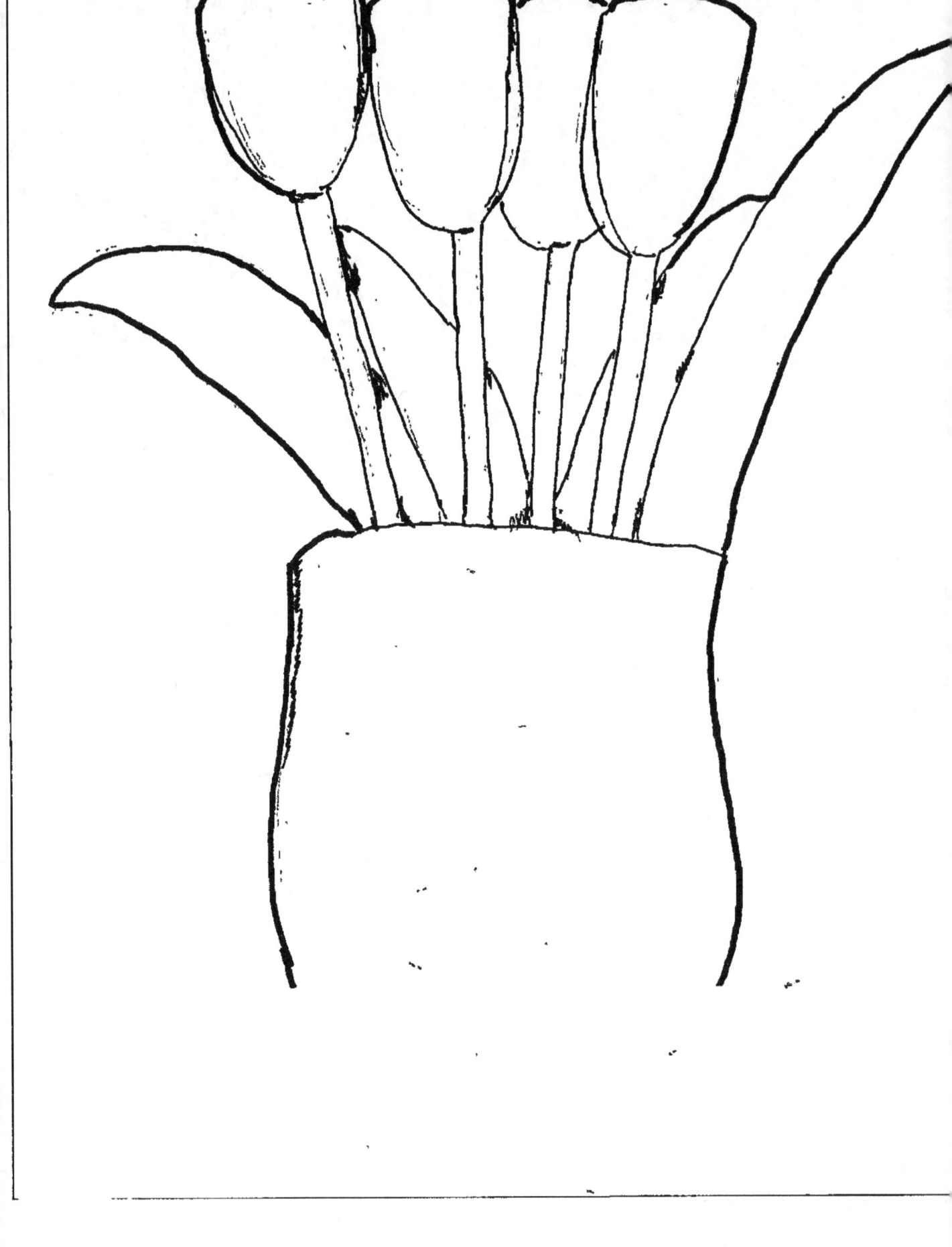

Many plants used water, sunlight, and surrounding elements to make their own food. However, some species used insects, small animals and/or fungi as food.

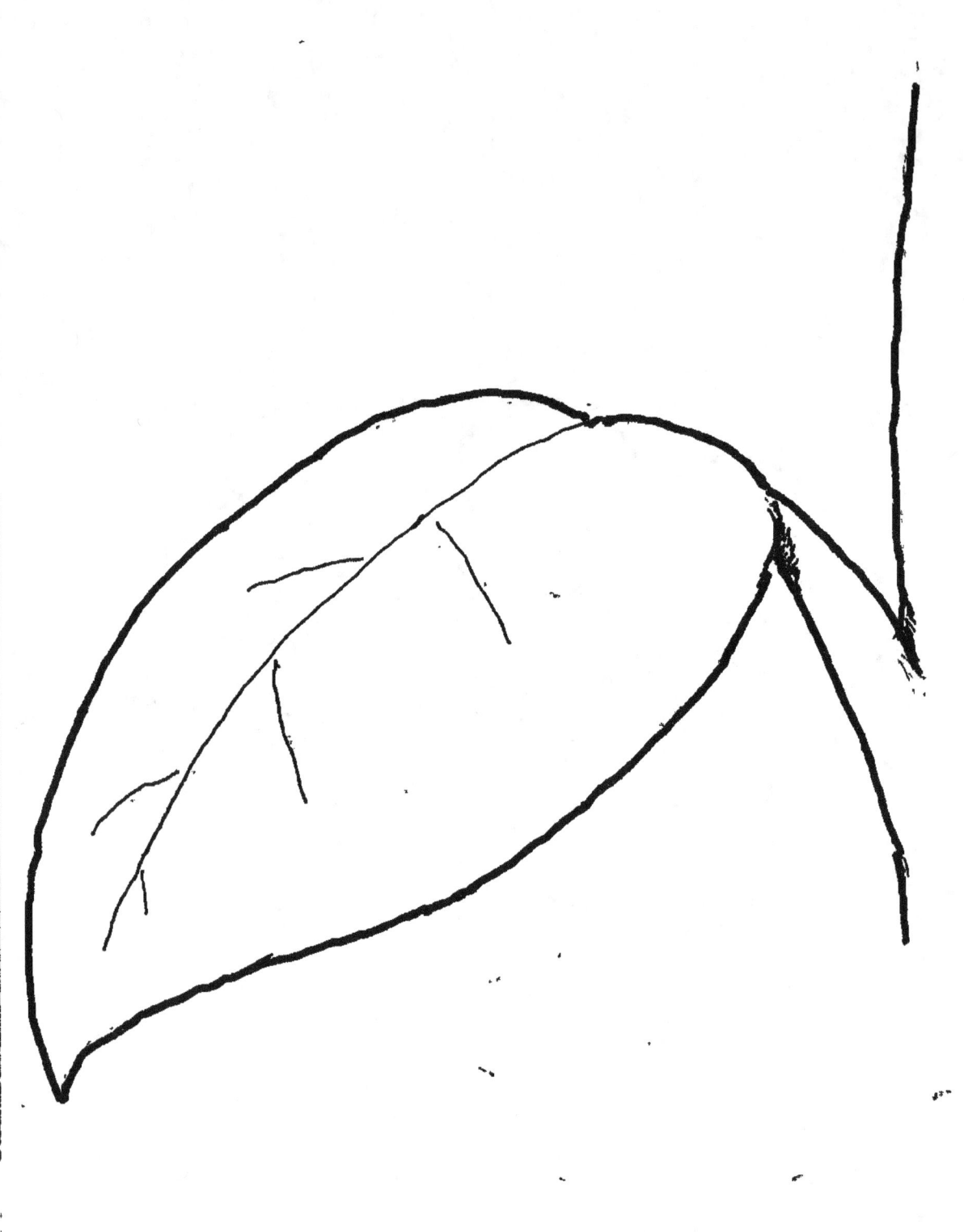

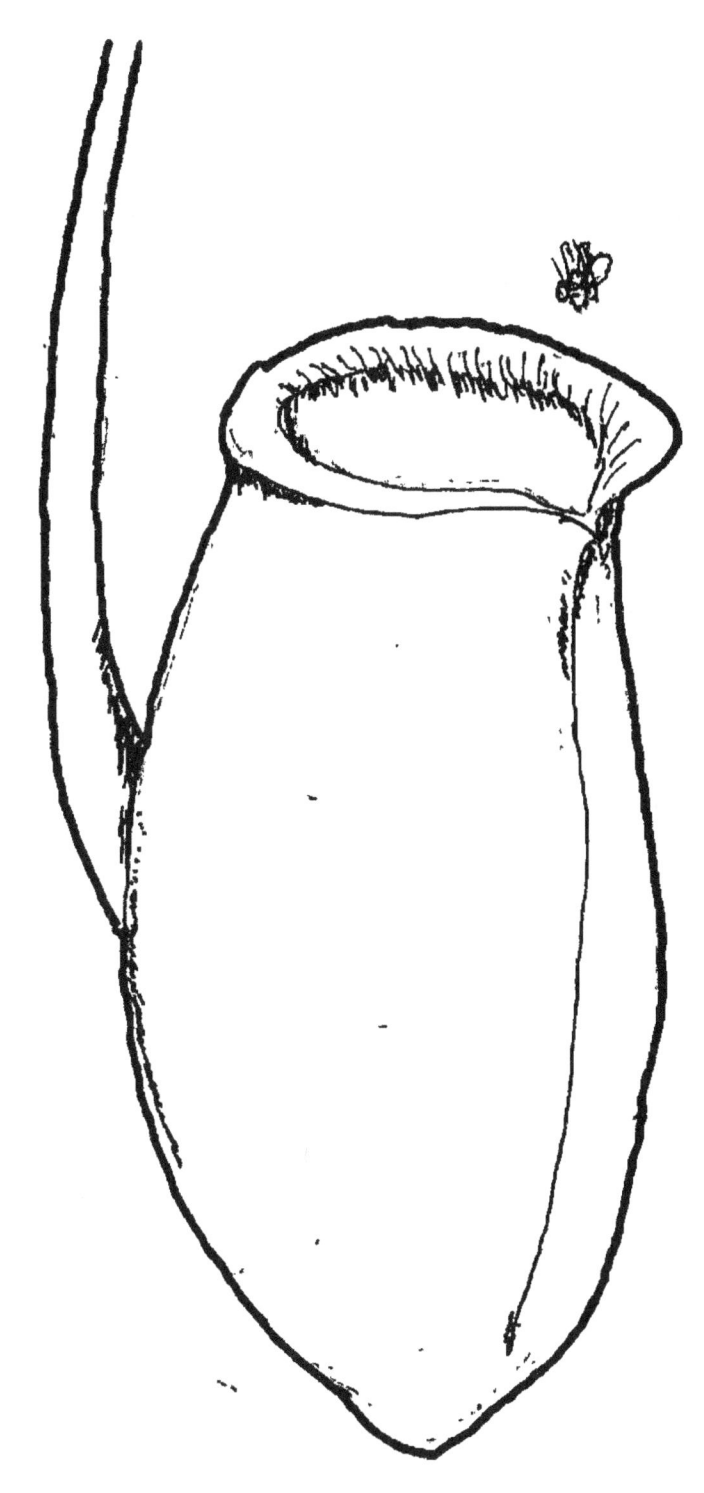

Plants reproduce through spores and/or seeds.

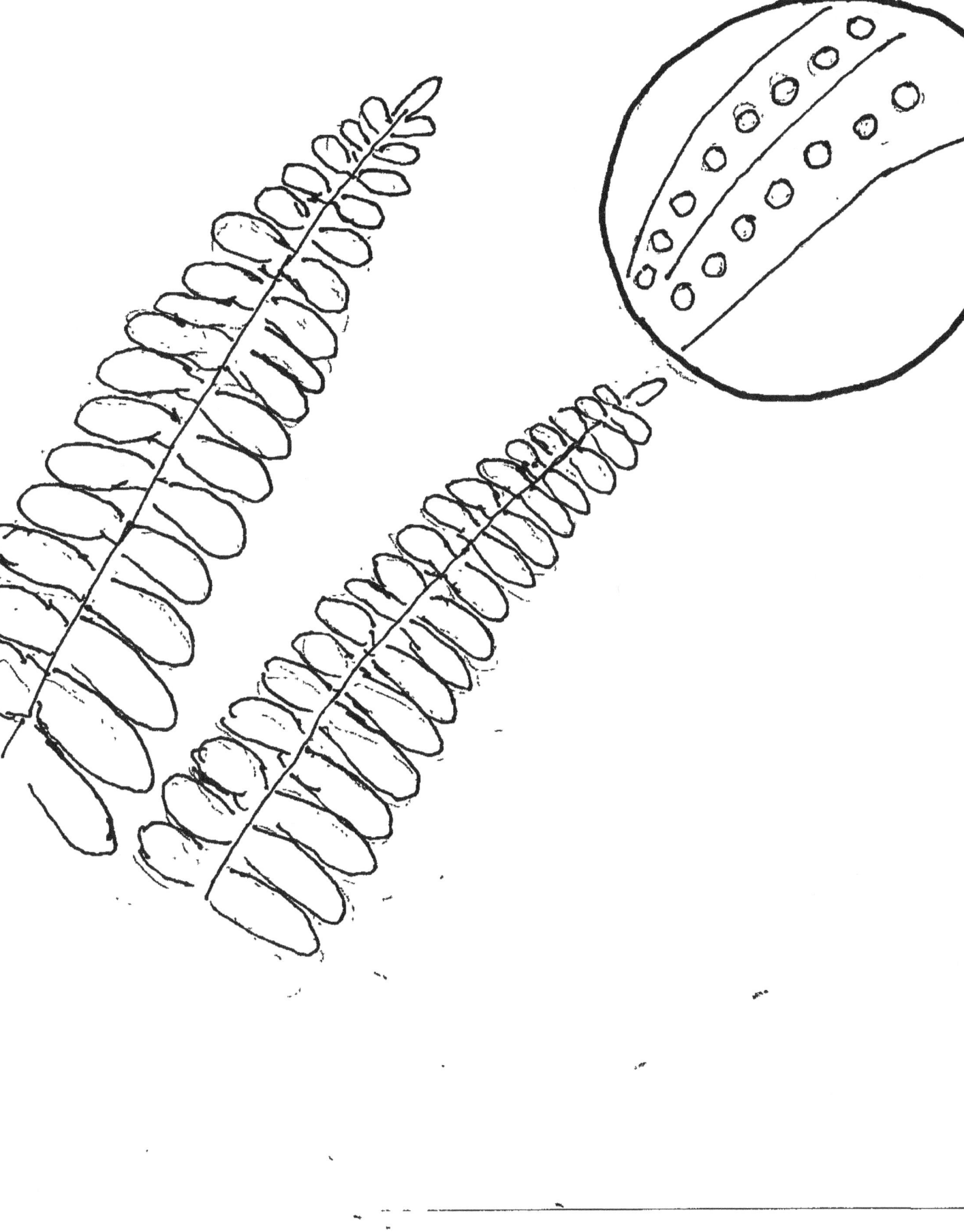

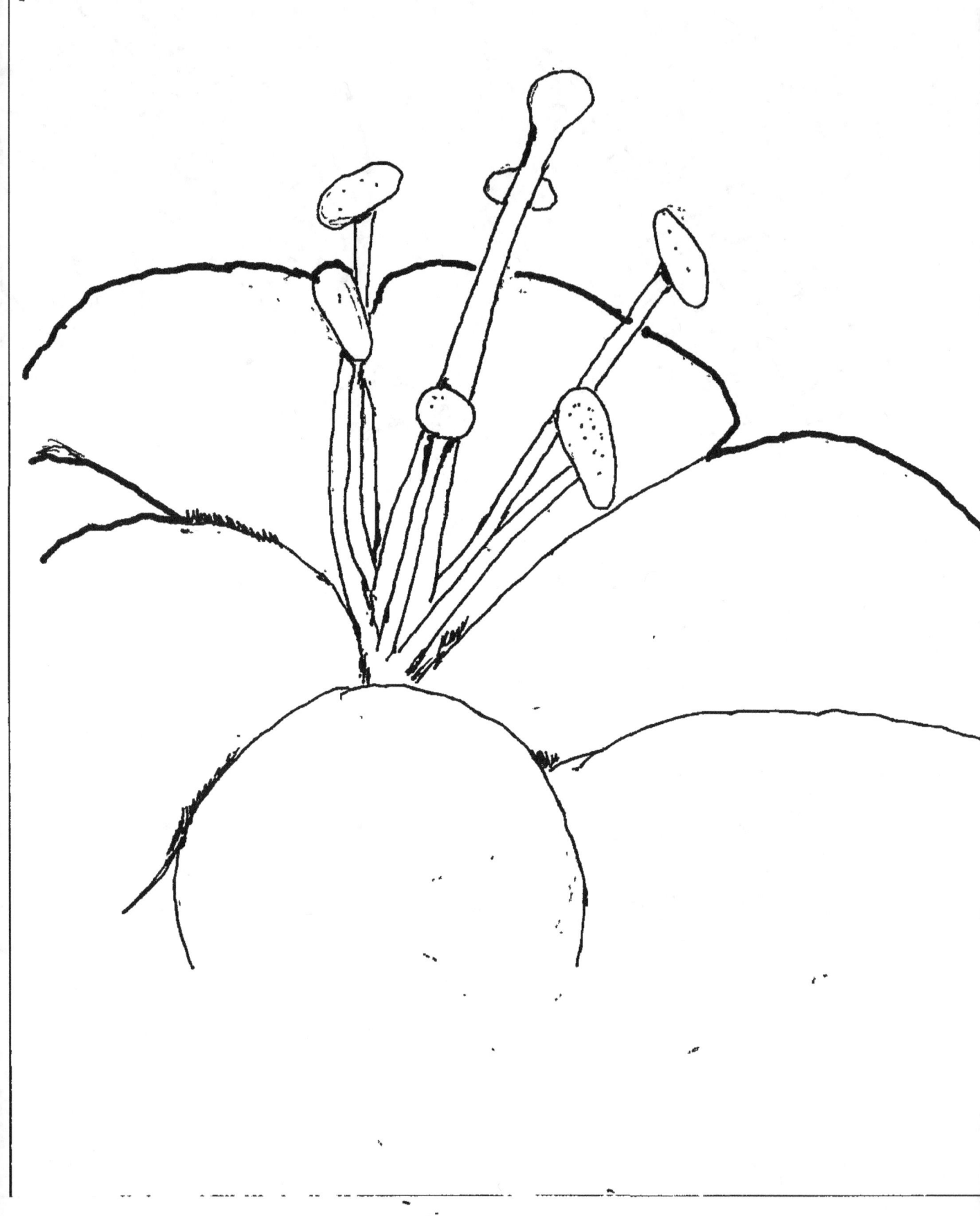

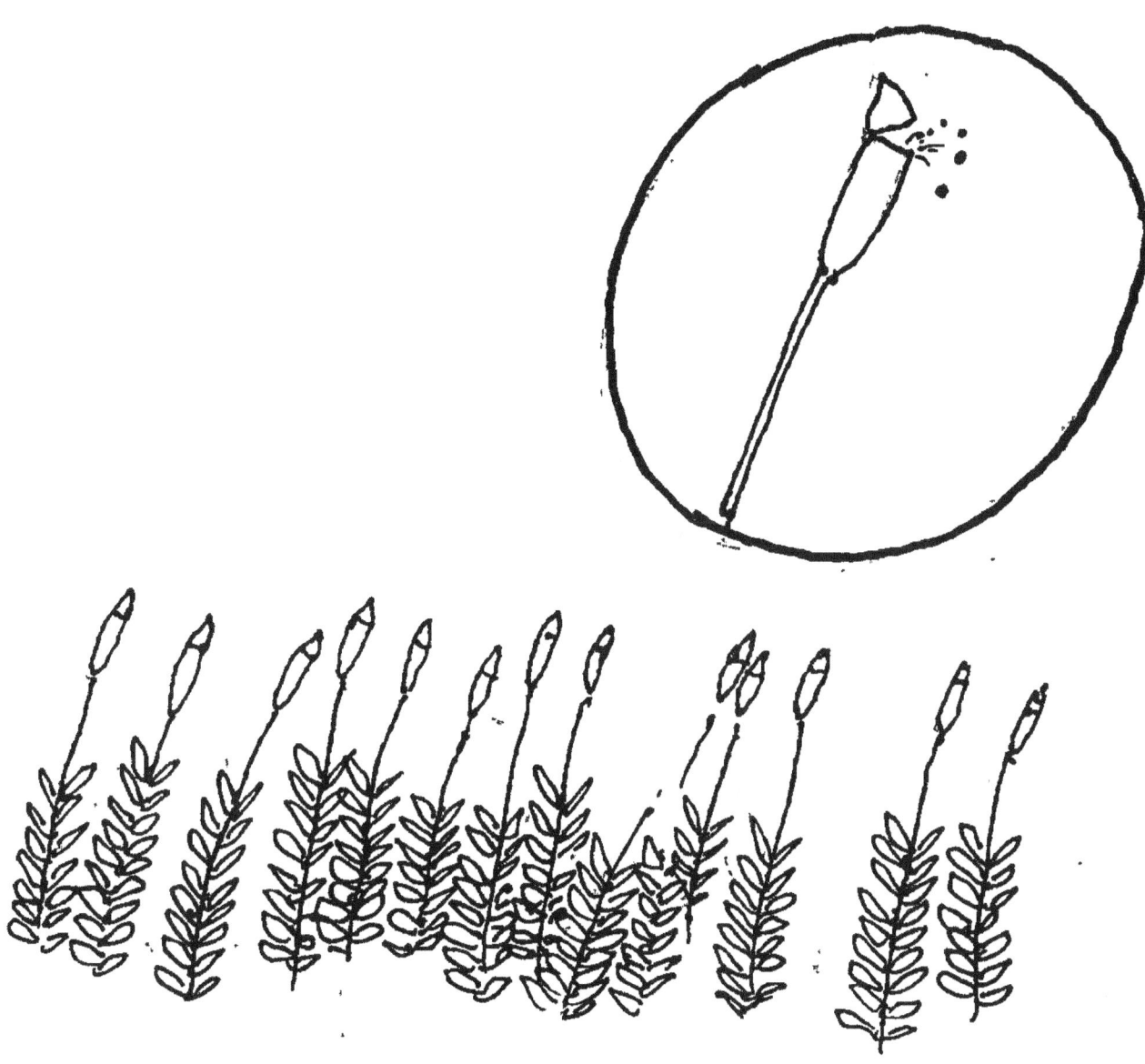

Plants lived on Earth, from the polar to the tropical regions of the planet.

Ferns, mosses, and flowers are some of the plants that lived on Earth.

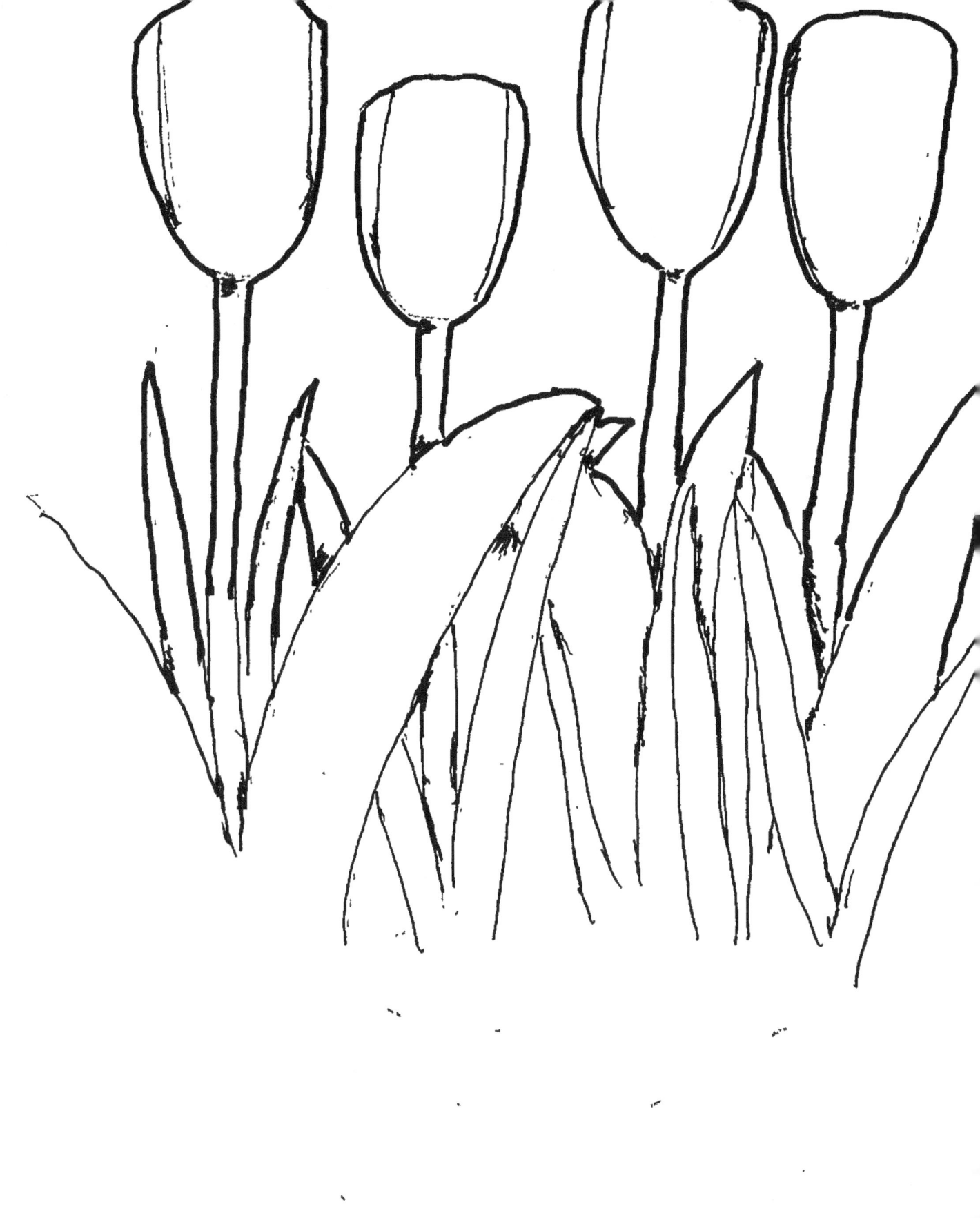

We use plants for our needs.

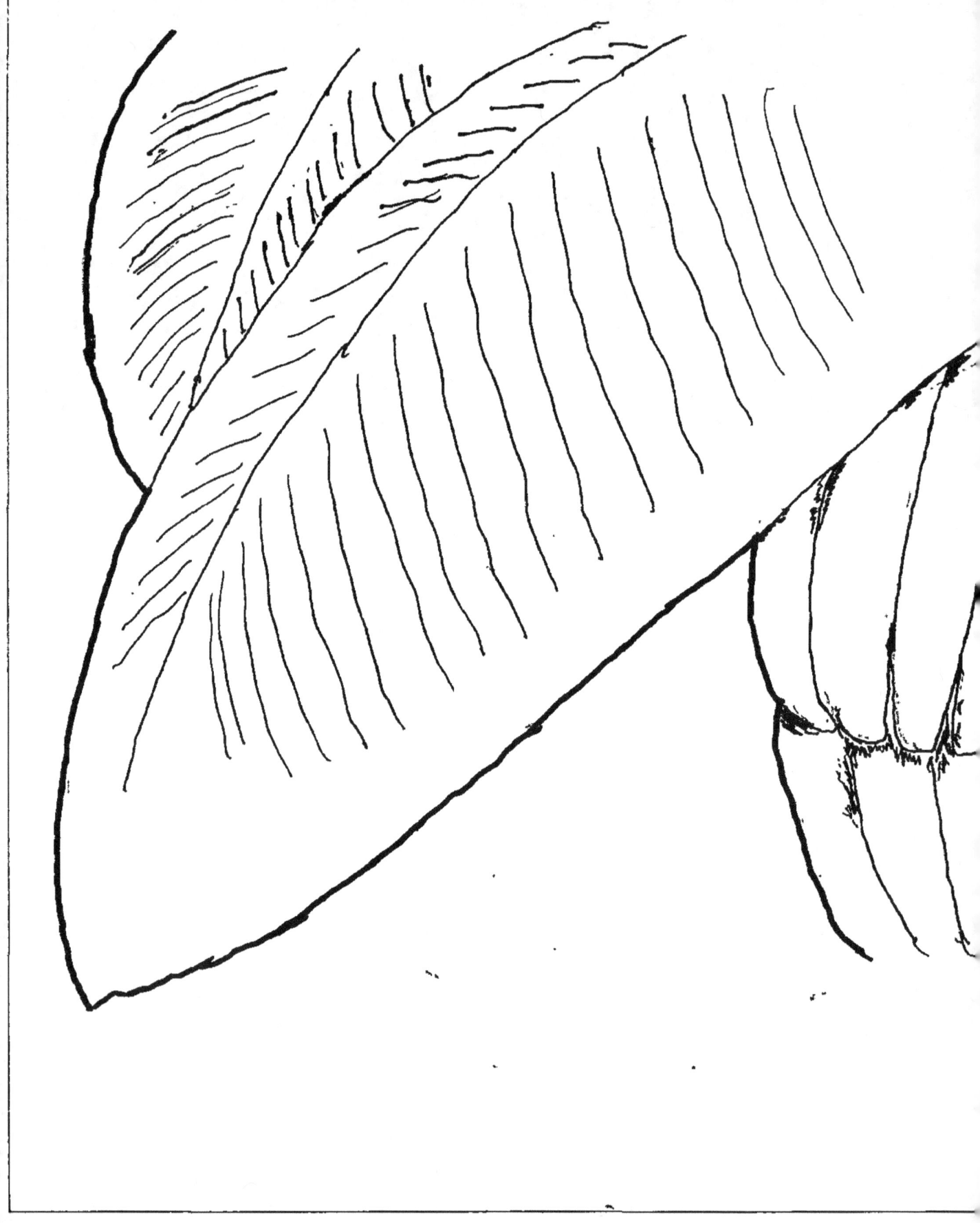

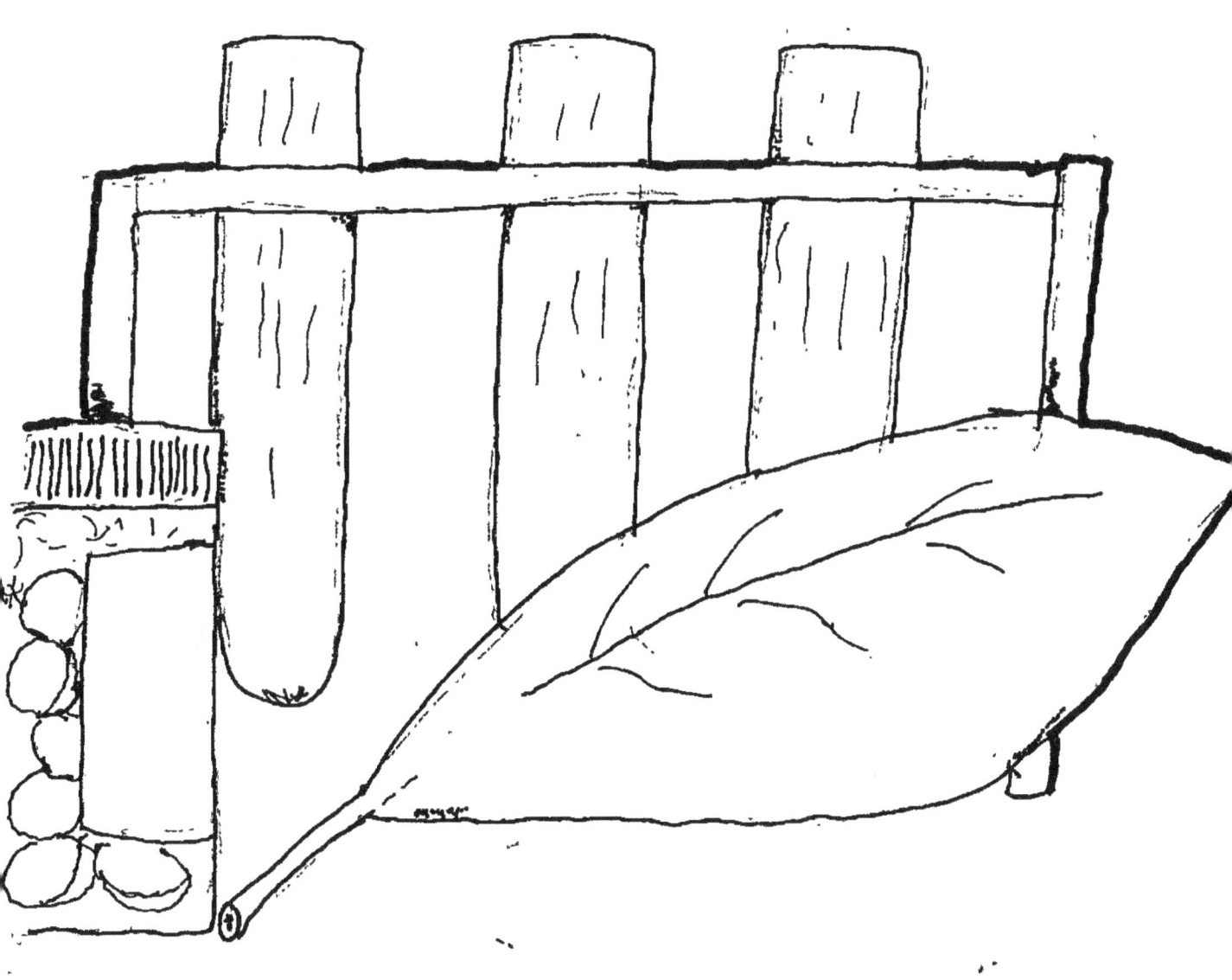

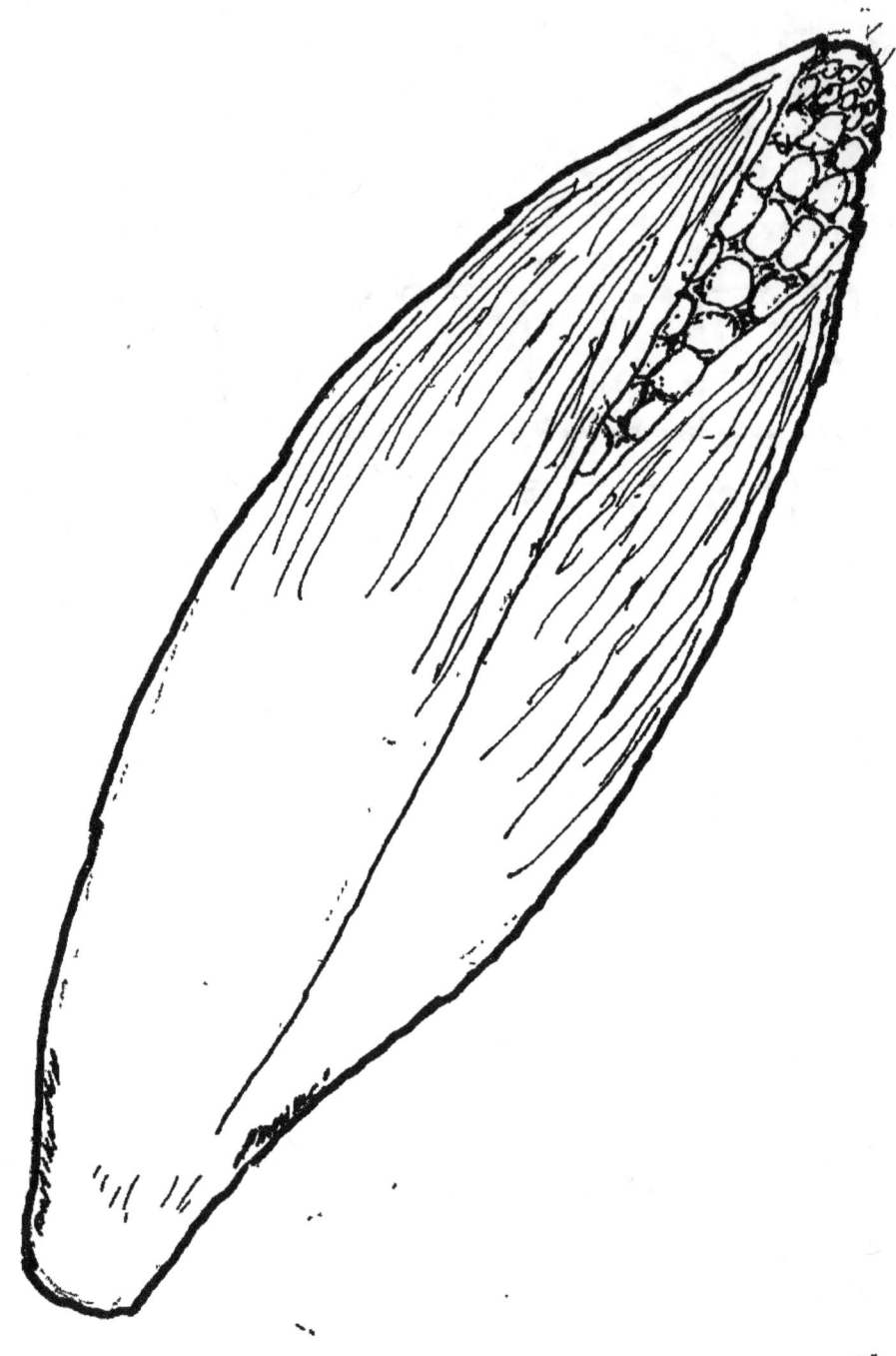

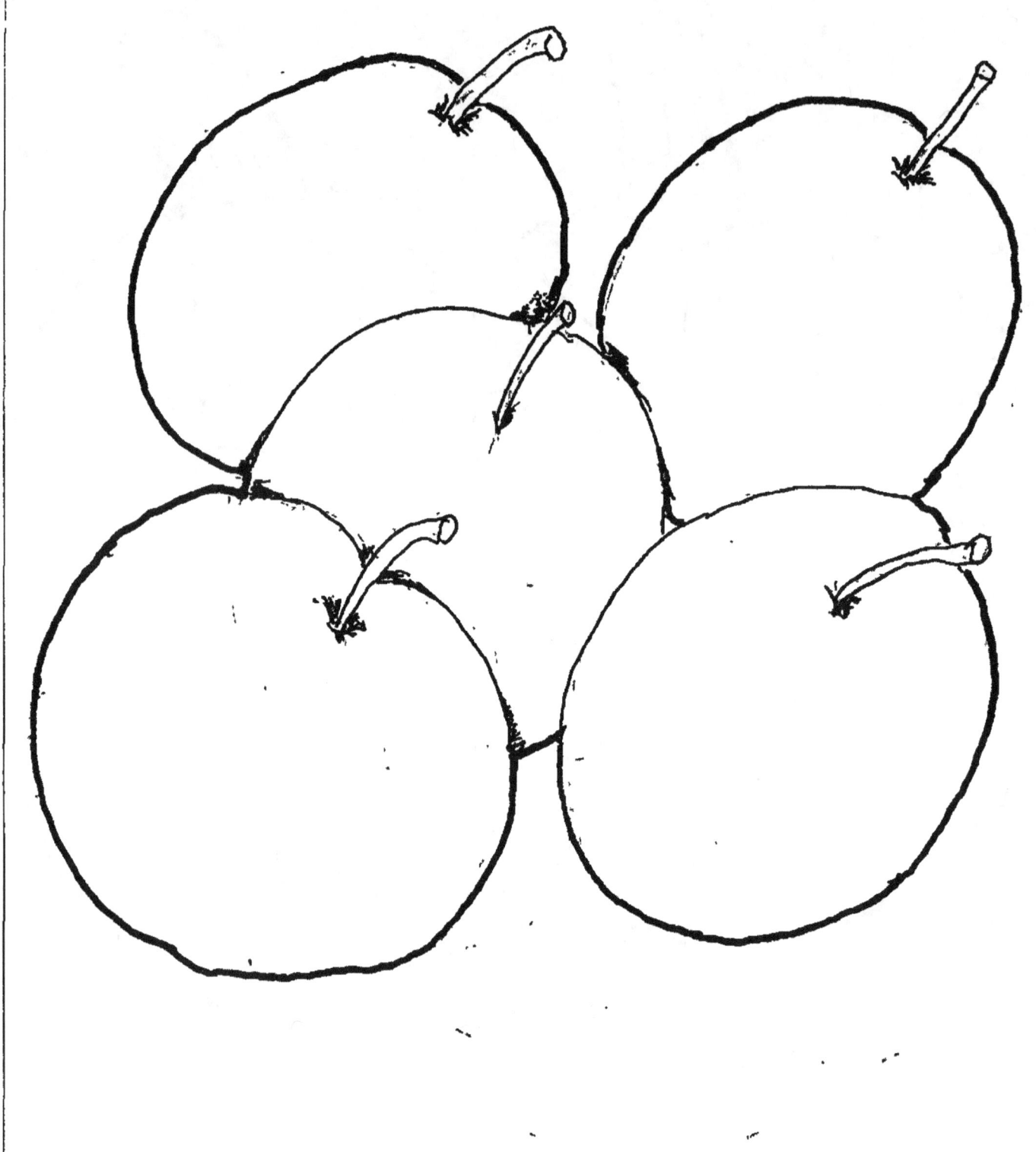

You can learn more about plants through many resources such as books, computers, and your teacher in school. However, we can turn to God for understanding about them.

Additional Resources

Ballard, Carol. Living Processes: Plant Variation and Classification. Wayland/The Rosen Publishing Group, Inc. New York. 2010.

Robinson, Richard Ed. Plant Science. Macmillan Reference USA; New York. 2001.

www.ingramcontent.com/pod-product-compliance
Lightning Source LLC
Chambersburg PA
CBHW081134280526
45787CB00007B/3074